Congressional
Research
Service

China's Political Institutions and Leaders in Charts

Susan V. Lawrence
Specialist in Asian Affairs

November 12, 2013

Congressional Research Service

7-5700

www.crs.gov

R43303

Summary

This report provides a snapshot of China's leading political institutions and current leaders in the form of nine organization charts and three tables. The report is a companion to CRS Report R41007, *Understanding China's Political System*, by Susan V. Lawrence and Michael F. Martin, which provides a detailed explanation of China's political system. This chart-based report is intended to assist Members and their staffs seeking to understand where political institutions and individuals fit within the broader Chinese political system and to identify which Chinese officials are responsible for specific portfolios. The information may be useful for Members and staff visiting China, hosting visitors from China, preparing for China-related hearings, or drafting China-related legislation.

Figures 1 and 2 depict China's political power structure as it was envisioned in Chapter 3 of the 1982 state constitution, and as actually implemented. The key difference is that while Chapter 3 of the state constitution identifies the National People's Congress as the highest organ of state power, the Communist Party of China exercises leadership over the entire political system.

Figures 3, 4, and 5 provide information about the Communist Party's leadership. Figure 3 presents the Party's hierarchy. Figure 4 lists the members of the Party's most senior decision-making body, the Politburo Standing Committee, and their portfolios. Figure 5 lists all 25 members of the full Politburo and their principal areas of responsibility.

Figure 6 lists the members of the Central Military Commission, a Party body that exercises unified command over the armed forces, known collectively as the People's Liberation Army.

Figure 7 shows where the largely honorary office of the State President sits within the state hierarchy, according to the state constitution. The president's authority actually derives from his concurrent post as General Secretary of the Communist Party.

Figure 8 presents the hierarchy of the State Council, a cabinet-like entity which is tasked with implementing Party policies and managing the state bureaucracy. China conducts its relations with most of the world through the State Council. Table 1 introduces the 10 members of the State Council Executive Committee, listed by rank, with information about each official's portfolio.

Figure 9 depicts the organizational structure of China's unicameral legislature, the National People's Congress.

Table 2 lists leading Party, military, and State officials with portfolios that include foreign affairs. Table 3 lists the top officials of China's Foreign Ministry, with information about each official's portfolio.

Contents

Figures

Tables

Contacts

Introduction

This report provides a concise, chart- and table-based introduction to China's political institutions and current leaders. The report is intended to assist Members and their staffs seeking to understand where political institutions or individuals fit within the broader Chinese political system and to identify which Chinese officials are responsible for specific portfolios. The information may be useful for Members and staff visiting China, hosting visitors from China, preparing for China-related hearings, or drafting China-related legislation. For a detailed discussion of the Chinese political system, see CRS Report R41007, *Understanding China's Political System*, by Susan V. Lawrence and Michael F. Martin.

China's Communist Party, which dominates the Chinese political system, convened its 18th National Congress in November 2012. At the Congress and a meeting immediately following it, the Party elected a new leadership to five-year terms ending in 2017. Xi Jinping became General Secretary of the Communist Party and Chairman of the Party's Central Military Commission, making him China's top leader for what is expected to be the next decade.

The first session of the 12th National People's Congress in March 2013 produced new leaders for the legislature, the State, the judiciary, the prosecutor's office, the State military commission, and other bodies. All such leaders were appointed to five-year terms ending in 2018. On this occasion, Xi Jinping assumed an additional post, as State President. A parallel meeting produced a new leadership for a high-profile political advisory body.

The charts included in this report reflect the structure of the Chinese leadership that emerged from those Party, legislature, and advisory body meetings.

All charts in this report were created by CRS.

All personal names are listed in Chinese style, with family names preceding given names.

China's Political Power Structure

China's current state constitution was adopted in 1982 and subsequently amended four times.[1] Its third chapter, entitled "Structure of the State," describes China's unicameral legislature, the **National People's Congress (NPC)**, as "the highest organ of state power." According to the state constitution, the NPC's role includes "supervising" the work of four other political bodies. They are listed below.

- The **State Council**. The state constitution describes it as "the highest organ of state administration"; it oversees the state bureaucracy and manages day-to-day administration of the country.

- The **State Central Military Commission**. The state constitution says it "directs the armed forces of the country."

- The **Supreme People's Court**. The state constitution calls it "the highest judicial organ."

- The **Supreme People's Procuratorate**. It is China's top prosecutor's office.

This political power structure is illustrated in **Figure 1**. The **Communist Party of China** is not mentioned in Chapter 3 of the state constitution, although Communist Party leadership is mentioned in passing five times in the state constitution's preamble.[2]

The Communist Party's own constitution provides more detail about Party leadership of the political system, the economy, and society at large, stating that "the Party commands the overall situation and coordinates the efforts of all quarters, and the Party must play the role as the core of leadership among all other organizations at corresponding levels." The Party constitution explicitly states that the Communist Party "persists in its leadership over the People's Liberation Army and other armed forces of the people."[3] The Party exercises that leadership through a **Party Central Military Commission**. It, rather than the State Central Military Commission, commands China's armed forces; the State Military Commission, which has identical membership to the Party Central Military Commission, is believed to exist in name only. In the Party constitution, Party leadership of the legislature, the State Council, the courts, and the prosecutor's office is not explicitly stated, but is implied. In practice, the Party nominates the leaders of all four bodies and operates Party committees within each of them. The courts and prosecutors' offices, the police, and some ministries report directly to Party Central Committee commissions and departments.

---

[1] The 1982 state constitution with all subsequent amendments incorporated into the text is available in English at http://english.gov.cn/2005-08/05/content_20813 htm.

[2] The clearest statement of Party leadership in the state constitution's preamble is, "*Under the leadership of the Communist Party of China* and the guidance of Marxism-Leninism, Mao Zedong Thought, Deng Xiaoping Theory and the Important Thought of the 'Three Represents,' the Chinese people of all ethnic groups will continue to adhere to the people's democratic dictatorship and the socialist road, persevere in reform and opening to the outside world, steadily improve socialist institutions, develop the socialist market economy, develop socialist democracy, improve the socialist legal system, work hard and self-reliantly to modernize the country's industry, agriculture, national defense and science and technology step by step, and promote a coordinated development of material, political and spiritual civilizations to turn China into a socialist country that is prosperous, powerful, democratic, and culturally advanced." (Italics are CRS'.)

[3] For an English-language version of the Party constitution, as revised and adopted on November 14, 2012 at the Party's 18th National Congress, see "Full Text of Constitution of Communist Party of China," Xinhua News Agency, November 18, 2012, http://news xinhuanet.com/english/special/18cpcnc/2012-11/18/c_131982575 htm.

Figure 2 provides an approximate illustration of China's power structure as currently implemented, with the Communist Party in charge.

Figure 1. China National-Level Political Power Structure as Described in Chapter 3 of the 1982 State Constitution

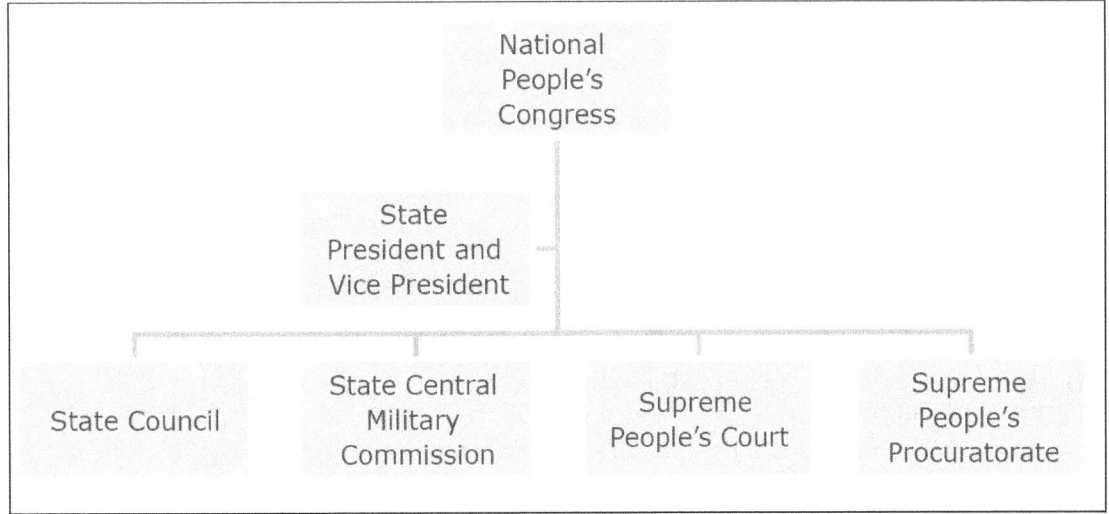

Source: "State Organs," Xinhua News Agency, http://news.xinhuanet.com/ziliao/2003-02/11/content_724234.htm.

Figure 2. China's Political Structure as Implemented

The Communist Party sits atop China's political power structure, controls all political institutions, and commands the military

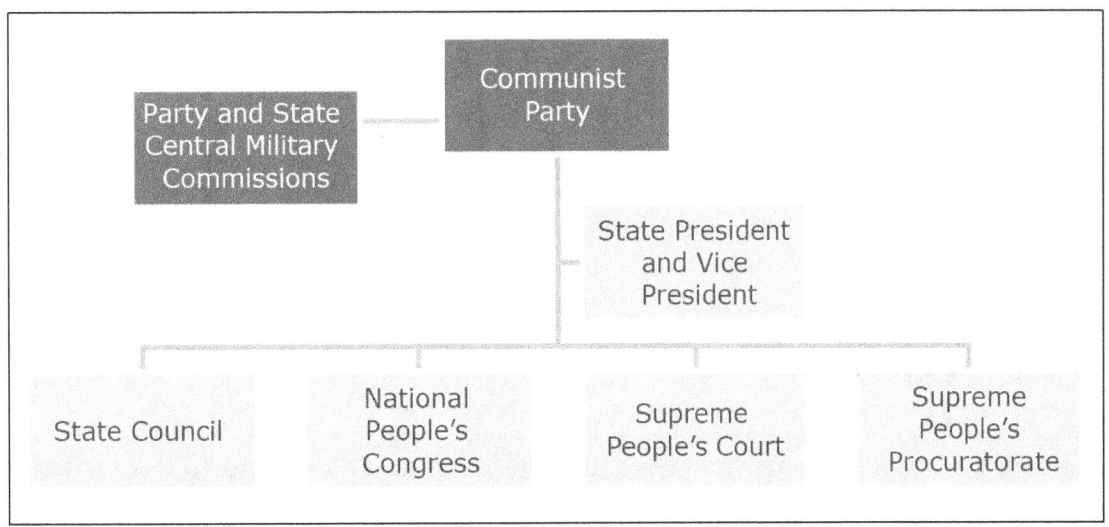

Source: CRS research.

The Communist Party of China (CPC)

With 85 million dues-paying members, just over 6% of China's population of 1.35 billion, the Communist Party of China (CPC) is the largest political party in the world.[4] As noted above, it is China's dominant political institution, exercising leadership over the entire political system.

The Communist Party constitution requires the Party to hold a national congress every five years. The most recent congress, the 18th, was held in November 2012. At each Congress, delegates elect a new **Central Committee** in a modestly competitive process: the Party leadership nominates approximately 10% more candidates than available positions. The current Central Committee is composed of 205 full members and 171 alternate members. They include 33 women (8.8% of the full 376-member Central Committee) and 39 ethnic minorities (10.4%).[5]

Each meeting of the Central Committee is known as a plenum. At its first plenum following a Party Congress, the Central Committee elects from among its members a 25-person **Politburo**, a more elite **Politburo Standing Committee**, which currently has seven members, and a **General Secretary**, who serves as China's top leader and who is required to be a member of the Politburo Standing Committee. These elections are believed to be non-competitive, with the outgoing Party leadership nominating only as many candidates as positions available. According to the Party constitution, the Standing Committee then nominates members of the **Party Secretariat**, which manages the daily operations of the Politburo and its Standing Committee and oversees Party Central Committee departments and commissions. Members of the Secretariat are subject to endorsement by the Central Committee. The Members of all the Party leadership bodies are elected or endorsed for five-year-long terms, until the next Party Congress.

The top officials in all non-Party institutions routinely hold concurrent Party posts, although they often do not publicize them. Party committees are embedded in the State Council, ministries under the State Council, the legislature, the courts, prosecutors' offices, state-owned enterprises, and all other public institutions, such as universities and hospitals, as well as in most private companies and many non-governmental organizations.

At the sub-national level, provinces, counties, and townships all have a Party committee and a parallel people's government, with the Party Secretary of the Party committee serving as the geographic unit's top leader.

---

[4] "截至2012 年底全国党员达8512.7万名" ("By the End of 2012, National Party Members Reached 85.127 Million"), *Xinhua Daily Telegraph*, July 1, 2013, http://news.xinhuanet.com/mrdx/2013-07/01/c_132499421.htm.

[5] For details of the election of the 18th Central Committee in November 2012, see Zhang Sutang, Qin Jie, Huo Xiaoguang, and Li Yajie, "十八届中央委员会委员选举差额比例为9.3%," ("The Ratio of Competitiveness for the 18th Central Committee Election was 9.3%"), *Xinhua News Agency*, November 15, 2013, http://politics.people.com.cn/n/2012/1115/c1001-19584526.html. At the 18th Party Congress, the outgoing Politburo offered delegates 19 more candidates than the 205 full Central Committee member positions available, and 19 more candidates than the 171 Central Committee alternate member positions available. The Party did not publicly release vote counts for individual candidates.

Figure 3. The Hierarchy of the Communist Party of China

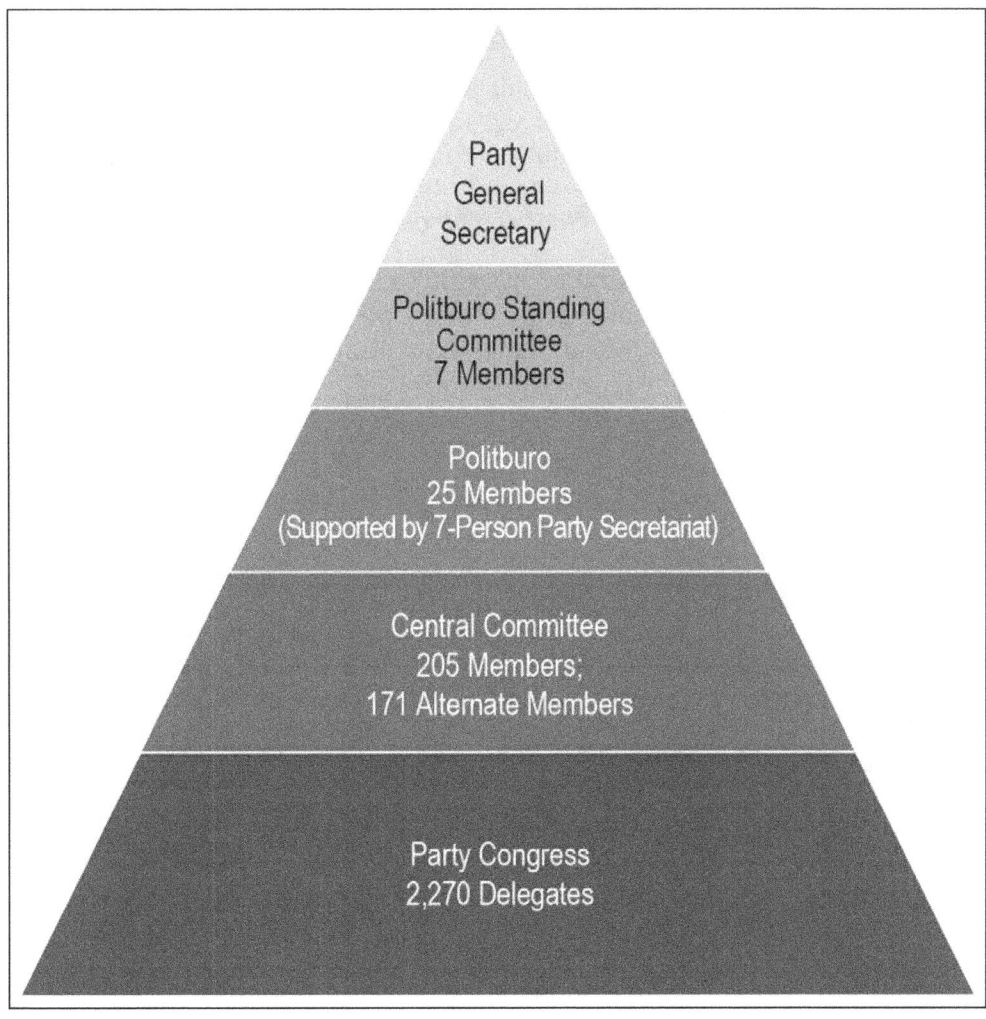

Source: Communist Party of China News Portal, http://cpc.people.com.cn/GB/64192/index.html.

The Communist Party Politburo Standing Committee

The Communist Party's Politburo Standing Committee (PSC) serves as China's most senior decision-making body. The Party constitution requires that Party committees at all levels of the Chinese political system operate according to "the principle of combining collective leadership with individual responsibility based on division of work."[6] Accordingly, each of the seven members of the PSC shoulders primary responsibility for a specific portfolio.

- The Party General Secretary serves concurrently as Chairman of the Party and State Central Military Commissions, which have identical memberships, and as State President. He also oversees foreign policy and, according to the Party constitution, has responsibility for convening Standing Committee and larger Politburo meetings and "presiding over" the work of the Party Secretariat.

- The second-ranked PSC member serves as Premier of the State Council, which manages the state bureaucracy. He is effectively China's top economic official.

- The third-ranked PSC member serves as Chairman of the Standing Committee of the National People's Congress (NPC), China's unicameral legislature.

- The fourth-ranked PSC member serves as chairman of a political advisory body, the Chinese People's Political Consultative Conference (CPPCC) National Committee. He is responsible for outreach to non-Communist groups, such as China's eight minor political parties, all of which pledge loyalty to the Communist Party, and state-sanctioned religious associations.

- The fifth-ranked PSC member heads the Party Secretariat, which oversees the Party bureaucracy. He also has responsibility for ideology and propaganda.

- The sixth-ranked PSC member heads the Party's Central Disciplinary Inspection Commission (CDIC), which polices the Party's ranks for corruption and other forms of malfeasance.

- The seventh-ranked PSC member serves as the top-ranked State Council vice premier and assists the Premier with his duties.

The collective leadership principle is generally understood to mean that the General Secretary must win consensus from his Standing Committee colleagues for major decisions.

Since 1997, China has evolved a set of age limits for top Party offices, although it is unclear if these are norms or rules. At the last three Party Congresses, in 2002, 2007, and 2012, no one older than 67 was appointed to a new term on the Politburo Standing Committee or the broader Politburo. Five of the seven Politburo Standing Committee members (all except Xi Jinping and Li Keqiang) and 6 of the 18 regular Politburo members will be over the age of 67 by the time the 19th Party Congress is scheduled to be held in 2017, and thus are expected to retire then. Barring unforeseen developments, Xi and Li are expected to be elected to new terms in 2017, retiring in 2022. Party and state leaders are limited to two five-year terms in the same position.

---

[6] "Full text of Constitution of Communist Party of China," Xinhua News Agency, November 18, 2012, http://news.xinhuanet.com/english/special/18cpcnc/2012-11/18/c_131982575.htm. The principle of collective leadership is presented in Chapter 2, Article 10 (5).

Figure 4. The Party Politburo Standing Committee (PSC)

Elected by the Central Committee in November 2012 for a five-year term

Xi Jinping	Li Keqiang	Zhang Dejiang	Yu Zhengsheng	Liu Yunshan	Wang Qishan	Zhang Gaoli
(b. 1953)	(b. 1955)	(b. 1946)	(b. 1945)	(b. 1945)	(b. 1948)	(b. 1946)
Party General Secretary	No. 2-ranked PSC member	No. 3-ranked PSC member	No. 4-ranked PSC member	No. 5-ranked PSC member	No. 6-ranked PSC member	No. 7-ranked PSC member
Chairman, Party and State Central Military Commissions	Premier and Party Secretary of the State Council	Chairman, Standing Committee of the 12th National People's Congress	Chairman, 12th National Committee of the Chinese People's Political Consultative Conference	Head, Party Secretariat	Secretary of the Central Disciplinary Inspection Commission	Vice Premier and Deputy Party Secretary of the State Council
State President				President, Central Party School		
Portfolio: Party, military, and State; foreign affairs	**Portfolio:** government administration and economy	**Portfolio:** legislative affairs	**Portfolio:** relations with non-communist groups	**Portfolio:** Party affairs, including Party bureaucracy and ideology	**Portfolio:** Party discipline and fighting corruption	**Portfolio:** assisting the Premier with government administration and economy

Source: Communist Party of China News Portal, http://cpc.people.com.cn; language on portfolios is based on CRS research.

Notes: All members except Xi Jinping and Li Keqiang are expected to retire at the 19th Party Congress in 2017. Barring unforeseen developments, Xi and Li are expected to serve until the 20th Party Congress in 2022.

The Communist Party Politburo

The full 25-member Politburo (or "Political Bureau") includes the seven members of the Politburo Standing Committee plus 18 regular members. Members whose primary area of responsibility is the Communist Party are the greatest in number, followed by members whose primary area of responsibility is the State, then the provinces, the military, the National People's Congress, and the political advisory body, the Chinese People's Political Consultative Conference.

Among the members whose primary area of responsibility is the Party, three preside over particularly sensitive portfolios, each considered by the Party to be crucial to maintaining Party rule. They are listed below.

- The head of the **Organization Department**, responsible for the recruitment of Party members and their assignment to jobs across the party and state, the legislatures, state-owned corporations, universities, and other public institutions.

- The head of the **Propaganda Department** (also known as the Publicity Department), responsible for the Party's messaging and for control of the media and ideology. In coordination with the Organization Department, the Propaganda Department manages the leaders of the Ministry of Culture; the General Administration of Press and Publication, Radio, Film, and Television; the Chinese Academy of Social Sciences; the People's Daily; the Xinhua News Agency; and other media organizations.[7]

- The head of the **Central Commission of Politics and Law**,[8] who oversees the security apparatus, including the courts, the prosecutors' offices, the internal and external state security bureaucracy, the police, and, in conjunction with the Central Military Commission and the State Council, the paramilitary forces.

The seven State positions that confer Politburo membership are the State President and Vice President, the Premier of the State Council, and the four State Council Vice Premiers.

The six geographic units represented on the Politburo include four municipalities with the same bureaucratic status as provinces: Beijing, Chongqing, Shanghai, and Tianjin. Also represented are the prosperous coastal province of Guangdong, next to Hong Kong, and the ethnic minority region of Xinjiang, in China's northwest. Two of the provincial leaders with seats on the Politburo, Guangdong Province Party Secretary Hu Chunhua and Chongqing Municipality Party Secretary Sun Zhengcai, are the youngest members of the Politburo. Because they have achieved high office at a young age, they are considered leading candidates for eventual promotion to Politburo Standing Committee membership.

The Politburo includes two women. They are Vice Premier Liu Yandong and Tianjin Municipality Party Secretary Sun Chunlan.

---

[7] For more information, see a brief introduction to the Propaganda Department's functions on the Communist Party of China's web portal, http://cpc.people.com.cn/GB/64114/75332/5230610.html.

[8] The commission is also known in English as the "Central Committee of Political Science and Law" and as the "Central Commission for Political and Legal Affairs."

Figure 5. The Party Politburo

Elected by the Central Committee in November 2012 for a five-year term; listed according to areas of primary responsibility

The Party	**Xi Jinping,*** Party General Secretary
	Liu Yunshan,* No. 5-ranked Member, Politburo Standing Committee; Head of Party Secretariat; President, Central Party School
	Wang Qishan,* No. 6-ranked Member, Politburo Standing Committee; Party Secretary, Central Discipline Inspection Commission
	Li Zhanshu, Member of Party Secretariat; Director of Central Committee General Office; Party Secretary of the Working Committee of the Organs Directly Under the Central Committee
	Liu Qibao, Member of Party Secretariat; Head of Central Committee Propaganda Department
	Meng Jianzhu, Secretary, Central Commission of Politics and Law; Director, Central Comprehensive Social Management Commission
	Wang Huning, Director, Central Committee Policy Research Office
	Zhao Leji, Member of Party Secretariat; Head of Central Committee Organization Department
The Military	**Xi Jinping,*** Chairman, Party and State Central Military Commissions
	Fan Changlong, Vice Chairman, Party and State Central Military Commissions; Army General
	Xu Qiliang, Vice Chairman, Party and State Central Military Commissions; Air Force General
The State	**Xi Jinping,*** State President
	Li Keqiang,* No. 2-ranked Politburo Standing Committee Member; Premier of the State Council; Party Secretary of the State Council Party Committee
	Zhang Gaoli,* No. 7-ranked Politburo Standing Committee Member; State Council Vice Premier; Deputy Party Secretary of the State Council Party Committee
	Liu Yandong, State Council Vice Premier; Member of the State Council Party Committee
	Li Yuanchao, State Vice President
	Wang Yang, State Council Vice Premier, Member of State Council Party Committee
	Ma Kai, State Council Vice Premier, Member of the State Council Party Committee
Provinces	**Guo Jinlong,** Party Secretary, Beijing Municipality
	Han Zheng, Party Secretary, Shanghai Municipality
	Hu Chunhua, Party Secretary, Guangdong Province
	Sun Chunlan, Party Secretary, Tianjin Municipality
	Sun Zhengcai, Party Secretary, Chongqing Municipality
	Zhang Chunxian, Party Secretary, Xinjiang Uyghur Autonomous Region and First Political Commissar of the Xinjiang Production and Construction Corps
National People's Congress (NPC)	**Zhang Dejiang,*** No. 3-ranked Politburo Standing Committee Member; Chairman, NPC Standing Committee
	Li Jianguo, Vice Chairman, NPC Standing Committee; Chairman, All-China Trade Unions
Advisory Body	**Yu Zhengsheng,*** No. 4-ranked Politburo Standing Committee Member; Chairman, National Committee of the Chinese People's Political Consultative Conference (CPPCC)

Source: Titles from the Communist Party of China News Portal, http://cpc.people.com.cn, and from Xinhua News Agency biographies. Grouping by areas of primary responsibility is by CRS.

Notes: Members of the seven-person Politburo Standing Committee are identified with asterisks. Xi Jinping leads the Party, the military, and the state, and so is listed in all three areas of responsibility.

The Communist Party's Military

The Party's **Central Military Commission** (CMC) exercises unified command over China's armed forces, consisting of the active and reserve forces of China's military, the **People's Liberation Army** (PLA); a paramilitary force, the **People's Armed Police Force** (PAP); and a militia. The PLA, with approximately 2.3 million active personnel and 510,000 reserves,[9] is not a national army belonging to the state. Rather, it serves as the Party's armed wing.

The civilian General Secretary of the Communist Party serves as the CMC's chairman. The rest of the CMC is currently comprised of uniformed officers. They are two vice chairmen (who serve concurrently on the Party's Politburo), the State Councilor for military affairs (who serves concurrently as Minister of Defense), the directors of the PLA's four general departments, and the commanders of the Navy, the Air Force, and the strategic and conventional missile forces, known as the Second Artillery Corps. The Party and State CMCs have identical memberships and are effectively a single body. The institution of the Party CMC is the locus of authority.

The responsibilities of the PLA's four general departments are listed below.[10]

- **General Staff Department:** operations, cyber and electronic warfare, communications/informatization, intelligence, training, force structure, mobilization, and foreign affairs;

- **General Political Department:** Communist Party affairs, personnel, military media and cultural troupes, and security;

- **General Logistics Department:** financial affairs and audits; housing, food, uniforms, and other supplies; military healthcare; military transportation; and capital construction; and

- **General Armament Department:** weapons and equipment needs, research and development, electronics and information infrastructure, and the manned space program.

The four general departments direct the service branches and serve as the national headquarters for the Army. They also direct China's military regions (MRs), also known as military area commands or theaters of war. The seven military regions are the Shenyang MR, Beijing MR, Lanzhou MR, Jinan MR, Nanjing MR, Guangzhou MR, and Chengdu MR. The Navy, the Air Force, and the Second Artillery Corps each has its own separate national headquarters. The Ministry of National Defense is not in the chain of command.

---

[9] "全国现役军人230万人 难以确定常住地人口4649985人" ("2.3 Million Active Service Military Personnel Nationwide; 4.649985 million People Whose Place of Permanent Residence is Difficult to Determine,") *Xinhua News Agency*, April 29, 2011. An April 2013 Chinese government White Paper reported that combat units in the PLA Army, Navy, and Air Force had a combined strength of 1.483 million personnel. Information Office of the State Council of the People's Republic of China, *The Diversified Employment of China's Armed Forces*, White Paper, April 16, 2013, http://www.china.org.cn/government/whitepaper/node_7181425.htm.

[10] "Structure and Organization of the Armed Forces," PRC Ministry of National Defense, http://eng mod.gov.cn/ArmedForces/index.htm. For more information, see Dennis J.Blasko, *The Chinese Army Today: Tradition and Transformation for the 21st Century*, 2nd ed. (New York: Routledge, 2012).

Figure 6. The Party Central Military Commission (CMC)

Appointed by the Central Committee in November 2012 for a five-year term

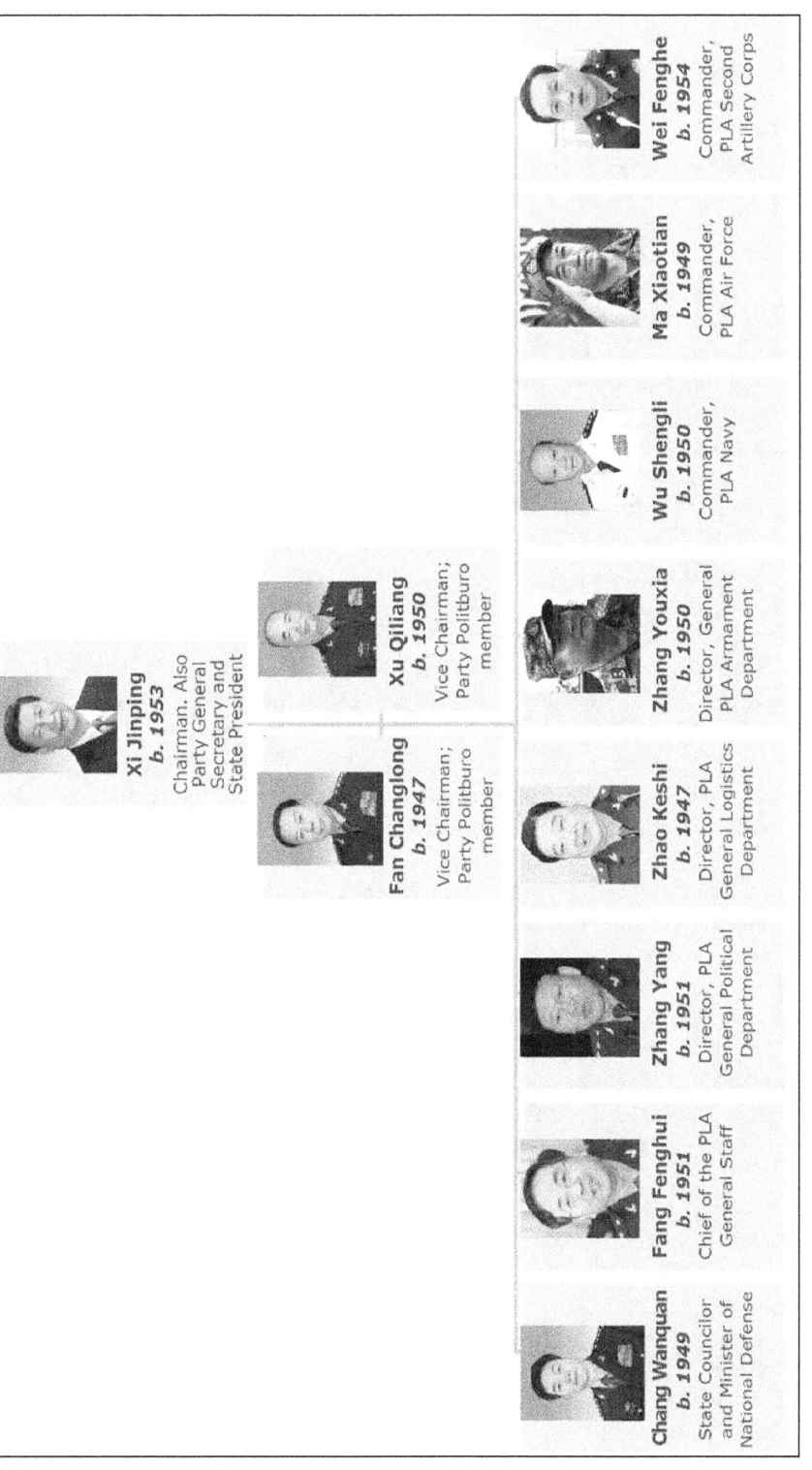

Xi Jinping
b. 1953
Chairman. Also
Party General
Secretary and
State President

Fan Changlong
b. 1947
Vice Chairman;
Party Politburo
member

Xu Qiliang
b. 1950
Vice Chairman;
Party Politburo
member

Chang Wanquan
b. 1949
State Councilor
and Minister of
National Defense

Fang Fenghui
b. 1951
Chief of the PLA
General Staff

Zhang Yang
b. 1951
Director, PLA
General Political
Department

Zhao Keshi
b. 1947
Director, PLA
General Logistics
Department

Zhang Youxia
b. 1950
Director, General
PLA Armament
Department

Wu Shengli
b. 1950
Commander,
PLA Navy

Ma Xiaotian
b. 1949
Commander,
PLA Air Force

Wei Fenghe
b. 1954
Commander,
PLA Second
Artillery Corps

Source: Communist Party of China News Portal, http://cpc.people.com/cn, and Xinhua News Agency biographies.

The State Presidency

The **State President** serves as China's head of state.[11] The position, held by Communist Party General Secretary Xi Jinping, is the highest State office, but is largely ceremonial and involves few duties. Since 1993, every Communist Party General Secretary has served concurrently as State President, largely to facilitate his meetings with other heads of state. As Communist Party General Secretary alone, he would have few counterparts.

Candidates for the positions of President and Vice President are nominated by the Communist Party and elected by deputies to the National People's Congress. So far, such elections have always been non-competitive. The Chinese government's official website states, however, that, "As the political democratization process continues, the single-candidate practice will gradually be replaced by multi-candidate election."[12]

According to China's state constitution, the President is subordinate to the National People's Congress (NPC). The actual power dynamic is reversed, because the position of the President is filled by the Communist Party General Secretary. The General Secretary/State President is the Party's top official, while the NPC Standing Committee Chairman is ranked third in the Party hierarchy for protocol purposes.

According to the constitution, the President promulgates laws that are passed by the NPC and ratifies treaties that are agreed to by the NPC. He nominates the Premier to the NPC, and appoints the Premier following NPC review. Following decisions by the NPC, the President is also responsible for officially proclaiming a state of emergency or a state of war and issuing mobilization orders. Other than appointing and, if need be, removing its top officials, the President officially has no role in the operations of the State Council, a separate political institution that oversees China's state bureaucracy.

The constitution decrees somewhat vaguely that the **State Vice President** "assists the president in his work" and "may exercise such functions and powers of the president as the president may entrust to him." The current Vice President, Li Yuanchao, is a regular member of the 25-person Politburo, but not a member of the elite seven-person Politburo Standing Committee. His Party protocol rank is lower than that of the State Council Premier and the top-ranked Vice Premier, who are both Politburo Standing Committee members. His rank is also marginally lower than that of the second-ranked Vice Premier.[13] President Xi is believed to have entrusted Vice President Li with a portfolio that includes substantial involvement in foreign affairs.

---

[11] A literal translation for the Chinese name for the office of state president would be "Chairman," but China's official translation is "President."

[12] "The Election of the President," www.gov.cn, the Chinese government's official web portal, http://english.gov.cn//2005-09/02/content_28476.htm.

[13] Like Vice President Li, the second-ranked Vice Premier, Liu Yandong, is a regular Politburo member. Vice Premier Liu is older than Vice President Li, however, and so is listed ahead of him in the rank-conscious state media.

Figure 7. The Presidency's Place in the Political Power Structure as Described in the State Constitution

In reality, the President has greater authority than the Congress Chairman or the State Council Premier because he serves concurrently as General Secretary of the Communist Party

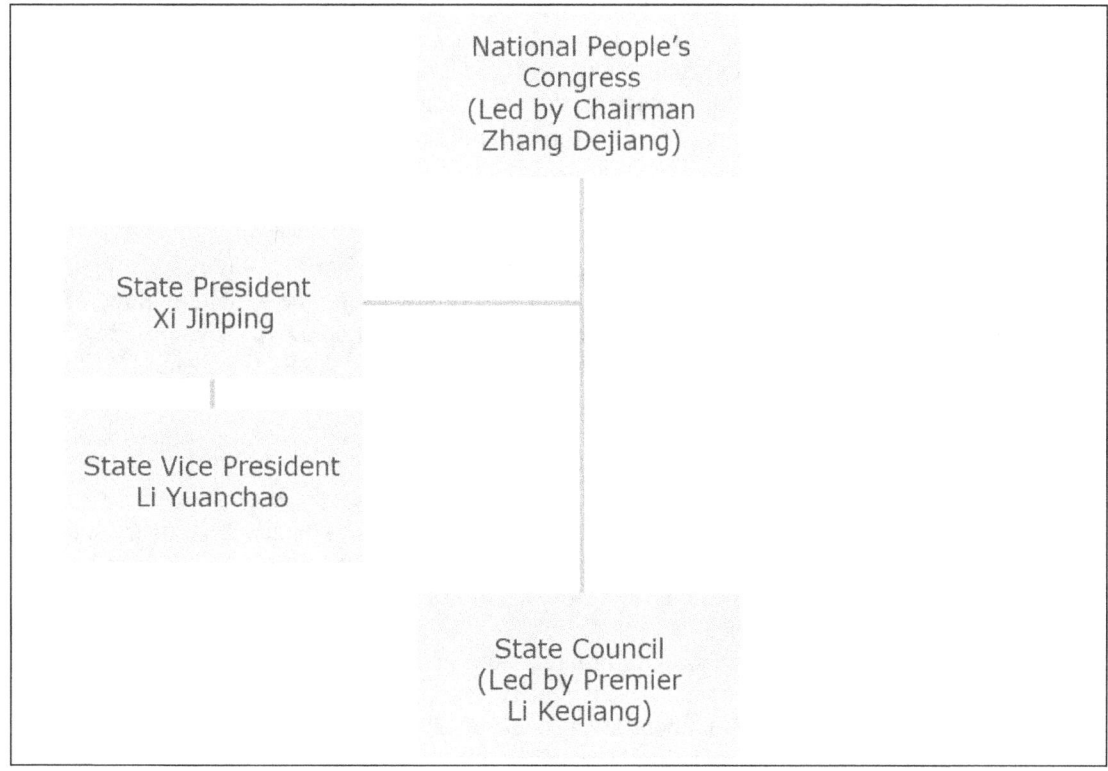

Source: "国家机构" ("State Organs"), Xinhua News Agency, http://news.xinhuanet.com/ziliao/2003-02/11/content_724234.htm.

The State Council

China's state constitution describes the State Council, also known as the Central People's Government, as "the highest organ of State administration." The State Council is officially responsible for implementing policies formulated by the Communist Party and laws passed by the National People's Congress, and for overseeing the day-to-day work of the State bureaucracy.[14] China generally conducts its external relations through the State Council.

The State Council is headed by a Premier, who serves concurrently as the Communist Party's no. 2-ranked official. He is appointed to his post by the State President, a position held by the Communist Party's top-ranked official. The Premier is assisted by four Vice Premiers, one of whom sits with him on the Party's Politburo Standing Committee, and the remaining three of whom are regular members of the Party's 25-person Politburo. Just below the Vice Premiers in rank are five State Councilors. State Councilors are full members of the Party's Central Committee, but do not hold seats on the more elite Politburo. The portfolios of all the Vice Premiers and State Councilors are described in **Table 1**.

The full State Council is akin to a cabinet. In addition to the Premier, the Vice Premiers, the State Councilors, and a Secretary General, it also includes the ministers of China's 20 ministries, the chairmen of three ministerial-level commissions, the governor of the central bank, known as the People's Bank of China, and the head of the National Audit Office.

Under the State Council are a wide array of organizations and administrative offices. They include such entities as the State-owned Assets Supervision and Administrative Commission of the State Council, which oversees national-level state-owned enterprises, and the State Administration of Taxation. They also include such entities as China's state news agency, Xinhua, and regulatory commissions for banking, securities, insurance, and electricity.

The State Council has the power to pass its own regulations and to draft legislation or authorize ministries to draft legislation, which it forwards to the National People's Congress for passage into law.

---

[14] In outlining the State Council's functions, the state constitution does not mention the State Council's role in implementing Communist Party policies. The Chinese government's official web portal, however, displays a Xinhua News Agency introduction to the State Council that describes the State Council as "responsible for carrying out the principles and policies of the Communist Party of China as well as the regulations and laws adopted by the NPC, and dealing with such affairs as China's internal politics, diplomacy, national defense, finance, economy, culture, and education." "The State Council," Xinhua News Agency, http://english.gov.cn/2005-08/05/content_20763 htm.

Figure 8. The Hierarchy of the State Council

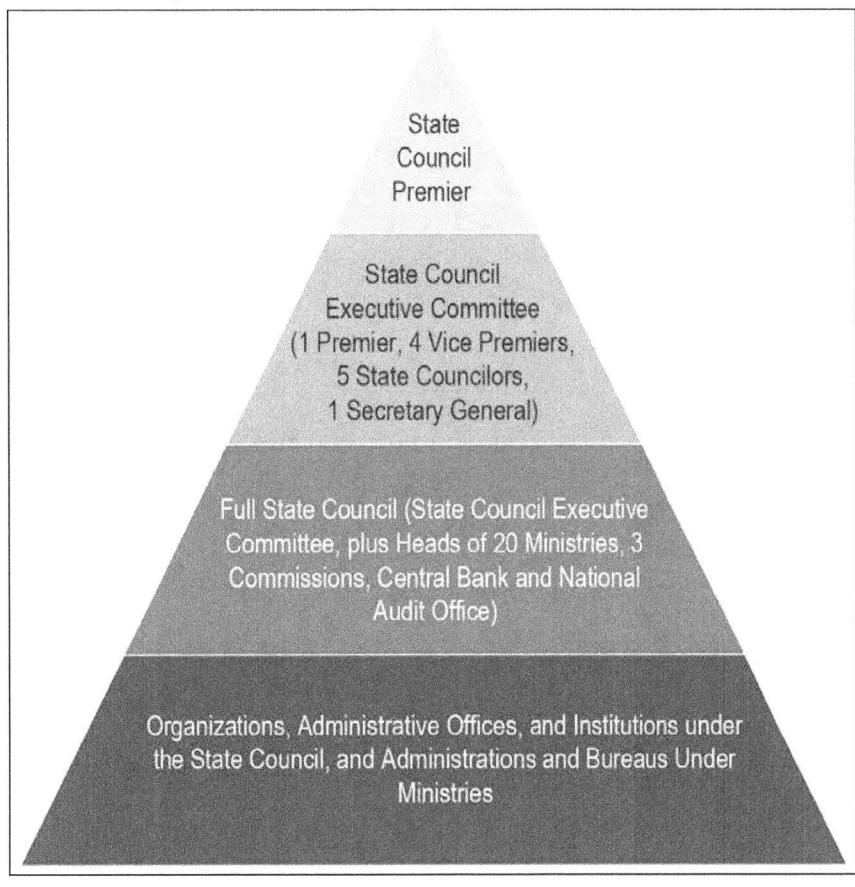

The State Council Executive Committee

The State Council's most senior officials are members of an Executive Committee composed of the Premier, four Vice Premiers, five State Councilors, and a Secretary General. The Vice Premiers are all members of the elite 25-person Communist Party Politburo, while the State Councilors are not. Because the current Secretary General serves concurrently as a State Councilor, the Executive Committee now has 10 members. Current Executive Committee members were appointed in March 2013 for a five-year term. They are listed below, along with their reported portfolios.

Table 1. The State Council Executive Committee

Name	State Council Title(s)	Other Titles	Birthdate	Reported Portfolio
Li Keqiang	Premier, Party Secretary of State Council Party Committee	No. 2-ranked Politburo Standing Committee member	July 1955	Government administration; economy
Zhang Gaoli	No. 1-ranked Vice Premier, Deputy Party Secretary of State Council Party Committee	No. 7-ranked Politburo Standing Committee Member	November 1946	Assisting the Premier; public finance; land and resources; environmental protection; housing
Liu Yandong	No. 2-ranked Vice Premier, Member of State Council Party Committee	Politburo member	November 1945	Education, science, culture (including media and publishing), health, and sports. Also serves as the Chinese co-chair of the U.S.-China People-to-People Exchange mechanism
Wang Yang	No. 3-ranked Vice Premier, Member of State Council Party Committee	Politburo member	March 1955	Agriculture, water resources, forestry, poverty alleviation, commerce, tourism. Also serves as the Chinese co-chair of the economic track in the U.S.-China Strategic and Economic Dialogue
Ma Kai	No. 4-ranked Vice Premier, Member of State Council Party Committee	Politburo member	June 1946	Financial sector, industry, transportation (including railway reform), human resources and social security

Name	State Council Title(s)	Other Titles	Birthdate	Reported Portfolio
Yang Jing	State Councilor; Member of State Council Party Committee; State Council Secretary General; Party Secretary of the State Council Organs Party Committee	Member of the Party Secretariat; Full Member of the Central Committee; Party Secretary of the Central State Organs Work Committee; President, Chinese Academy of Governance	December 1953	State Council affairs; liaison for the Premier with the Ministry of Supervision, State Auditor General, and the State Council Research Office; ethnic minorities and religious policy
Chang Wanquan	State Councilor; Member of State Council Party Committee; Minister of National Defense	Full Member of the Central Committee; Member of Party and State Central Military Commissions	January 1949	Defense foreign affairs and mobilization work
Yang Jiechi	State Councilor, Member of State Council Party Committee	Full Member of the Central Committee; Office Director, Foreign Affairs Leading Small Group	May 1950	Foreign Affairs; policy toward ethnic Chinese living abroad; Hong Kong, Macau and Taiwan affairs
Guo Shengkun	State Councilor; Member of State Council Party Committee; Minister and Party Secretary of Ministry of Public Security; Commissioner General of Police	Full Member of the Central Committee; Deputy Party Secretary, Central Commission of Politics and Law	October 1954	Public security, judicial bodies, state security
Wang Yong	State Councilor, Member of State Council Party Committee	Full Member of the Central Committee	December 1955	State-owned enterprises, work safety, quality inspection, commerce

Sources: "The Central People's Government of the People's Republic of China," http://www.gov.cn/gjjg/2005-08/01/content_18608.htm; Ma Haoliang 马浩亮, "新一届国务院领导分工确定 马凯主管工业" ("New State Council Leaders Portfolios Confirmed; Ma Kai Will Oversee Industry"), April 16, 2013, http://news.takungpao.com/mainland/zgzq/2013-04/1549650.html; "国务委员王勇分管国资、安监、工商等领域" ("State Councilor Wang Yong is in Charge of State Enterprises, Work Safety, and Commerce"), *Takung Pao*, May 3, 2013, http://news.takungpao.com/mainland/zgzq/2013-05/1586796.html; Yang Jiechi, "Innovation in China's Foreign Policy Theory and Practice Under the New Situation" (in Chinese), *Seeking Truth (Qiushi)*, August 16, 2013, http://www.qstheory.cn/zxdk/2013/201316/201308/t20130813_259197.htm.

Notes: Information about portfolios is drawn from reports in Beijing-backed Hong Kong media. China does not typically announce the portfolios of its top officials.

The National People's Congress

The National People's Congress is China's unicameral legislature. China's 1982 state constitution describes the NPC as "the highest organ of state power." The state constitution gives the NPC the power to amend the state constitution; supervise its enforcement; enact and amend laws; ratify and abrogate treaties; approve the state budget and plans for national economic and social development; and elect and impeach top officials of the state and judiciary. It also authorizes the NPC to supervise the work of the State Council, the State Central Military Commission, the Supreme People's Court, and the chief prosecutor's office, known as the Supreme People's Procuratorate. In reality, the NPC is controlled by the Communist Party and exercises many of its constitutionally conferred powers in name only.

Each Congress lasts five years. The current Congress, the 12th NPC, began in March 2013. The full Congress is composed of approximately 3,000 delegates. They are nominated by the Communist Party and elected by 35 electoral units: the people's congresses of 22 provinces, 5 autonomous regions, and 4 provincial-level cities, plus election councils for the People's Liberation Army, the Hong Kong and Macao Special Administrative Regions, and "Taiwan compatriots." The full Congress meets for a single annual session of about 10 days every March. Because the full Congress's annual session is so brief, much of the NPC's work is undertaken by its **Standing Committee**, which currently has 161 members and convenes every two months. The NPC's highest-ranking official is the Chairman of the Standing Committee, who serves concurrently as the Communist Party's no. 3-ranked official. Many of the NPC's top officials are retired senior officials from other parts of the political system who are able to extend their political careers by up to 10 years by serving in the Congress.

Nine **NPC specialized committees**, composed of deputies, meet throughout the year, usually once a month. They do not have the power to amend legislation assigned to them for review, or to approve personnel for other constitutional branches of government. They do have a formal role, however, in offering advice on legislation to the Standing Committee and the full Congress and performing oversight. Because the NPC does not have a specialized committee specifically focused on military affairs, the **Foreign Affairs Committee** is responsible for advising on legislation on both foreign affairs and defense matters. The Foreign Affairs Committee also has responsibility for international parliamentary exchanges.

Five institutions composed of staff and outside experts support the Standing Committee. A sixth institution supporting the Standing Committee, the Deputy Credential Examination Committee, is composed of NPC delegates.

Figure 9. The National People's Congress

Includes 9 specialized committees of deputies (in blue) and 6 bodies that support the work of the NPC Standing Committee (in yellow)

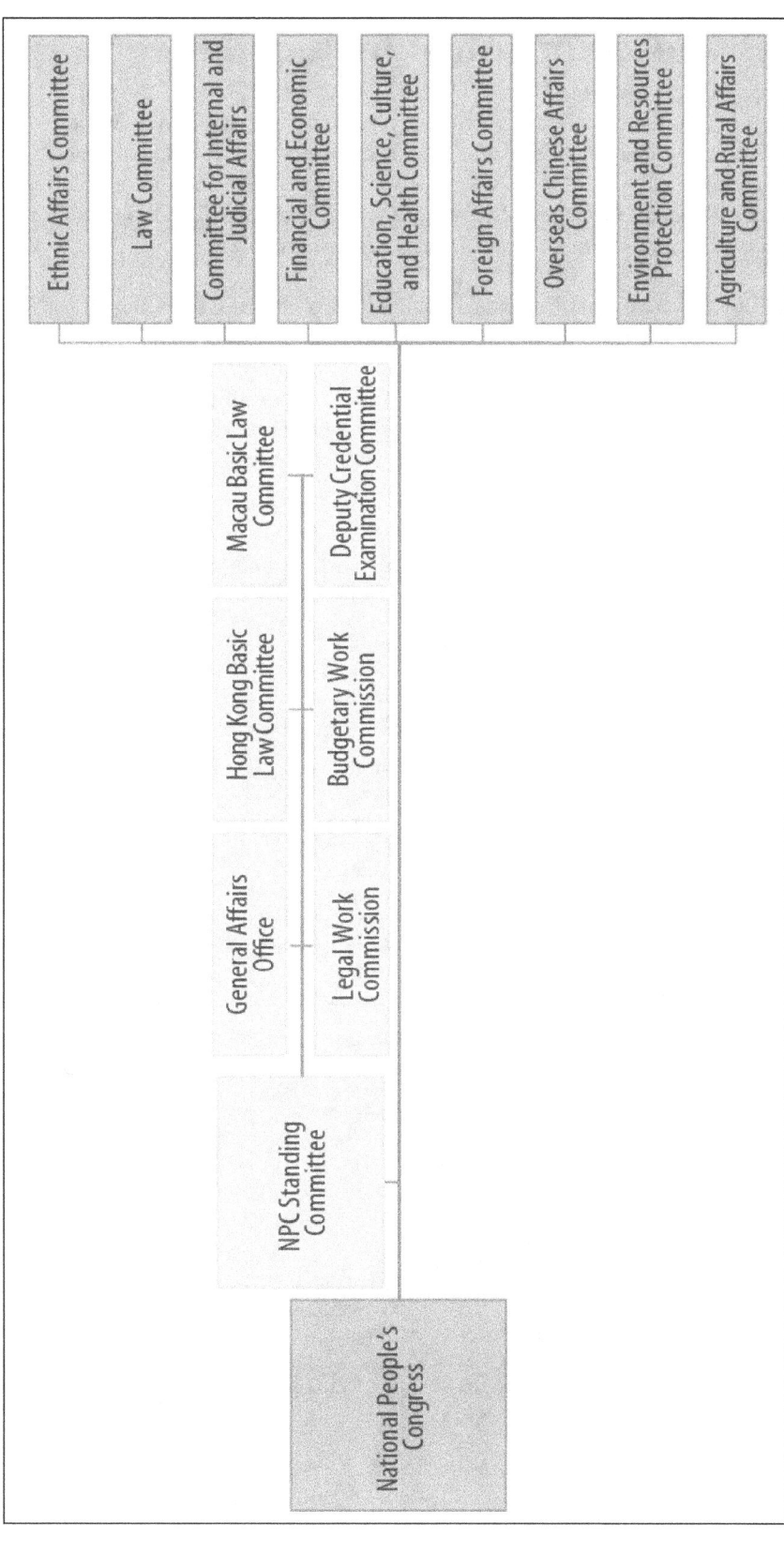

Source: "全国人民代表大会" ("National People's Congress"), Xinhua News Agency, http://news.xinhuanet.com/ziliao/2004-11/15/content_2221419.htm.

Officials Whose Portfolios Include Foreign Affairs

Several members of the 25-person Party Politburo have portfolios that include foreign affairs. The most prominent are President Xi Jinping and Vice President Li Yuanchao, who are believed to serve as the head and deputy head of the Party's coordinating body for foreign affairs, the Central Committee Foreign Affairs Leading Small Group. (The group's membership is not publicly disclosed.) No Politburo member focuses full-time on foreign policy.

China's top diplomat, State Councilor Yang Jiechi, is one of 205 full members of the Party Central Committee, but is not a member of the Politburo. China's Foreign Minister, Wang Yi, also a Central Committee member, is subordinate to State Councilor Yang. In managing China's foreign policy, the State Councilor for Foreign Affairs and the Foreign Minister must contend with other foreign policy players from the military, the propaganda apparatus, the security organs, the Ministry of Commerce, and the bureaucracies responsible for Taiwan, Hong Kong, Macao, and "overseas Chinese" affairs.

Table 2. Select Leading Party, Military, State, and Legislative Officials with Foreign Affairs Portfolios

Area of Responsibility	Name	Foreign Affairs-Related Position(s)	(Other) Communist Party Titles	Birthdate	Portfolio
Party/Presidency/ Military	**Xi Jinping**	State President; Head, Party Central Committee Foreign Affairs Leading Small Group	Party General Secretary; No. 1-ranked Member, Party Politburo Standing Committee; Full Member of Party Central Committee	June 1953	The Party, the military, and the state; foreign affairs
Vice Presidency	**Li Yuanchao**	State Vice President; Presumed Deputy Head, Party Central Committee Foreign Affairs Leading Small Group	Member, Party Politburo; Full Member of Party Central Committee	November 1950	Assisting the President, including with foreign affairs
Overall Diplomacy	**Yang Jiechi**	State Councilor for foreign affairs; Director, Office of the Party Central Committee Foreign Affairs Leading Small Group	Full Member of Party Central Committee	May 1950	Full-time management of foreign affairs, including supervision of the Ministry of Foreign Affairs

Area of Responsibility	Name	Foreign Affairs-Related Position(s)	(Other) Communist Party Titles	Birthdate	Portfolio
Foreign Ministry	**Wang Yi**	Minister and Presumed Deputy Party Secretary, Ministry of Foreign Affairs	Full Member of Party Central Committee	October 1953	Foreign affairs
Party Diplomacy	**Wang Jiarui**	Head, Party Central Committee International Liaison Department; Vice Chairman, National Committee of the Chinese People's Political Consultative Conference	Full Member of Party Central Committee	September 1949	International party-to-party relations
Military	**Chang Wanquan** (Army General)	State Councilor for military affairs; Minister of National Defense	Full Member of Party Central Committee; 4th-ranked Member, Party Central Military Commission	January 1949	Chinese military's interactions with foreign militaries
Military	**Sun Jianguo** (Navy Admiral)	Deputy Chief of the People's Liberation Army General Staff Department	Full Member of Party Central Committee	February 1952	Military intelligence
Military	**Wang Guanzhong** (Army Lieutenant General)	Deputy Chief of the People's Liberation Army General Staff Department	Full Member of the Party Central Committee	February 1953	Military foreign affairs
Party/Propaganda	**Liu Yunshan**	Politburo Standing Committee member with responsibility for propaganda and ideology, as well as managing the Party bureaucracy	Head (No. 1-ranked Secretary), Party Secretariat; Full Member of the Party Central Committee; Director, Central Guidance Commission for Building Spiritual Civilization	July 1947	Oversight of propaganda and ideology; management of Central Committee Departments, including the International Liaison Department

Area of Responsibility	Name	Foreign Affairs-Related Position(s)	(Other) Communist Party Titles	Birthdate	Portfolio
Propaganda	**Liu Qibao**	Head, Party Central Committee Propaganda Department	Member, Party Politburo; Member, Party Secretariat; Full Member of Party Central Committee	January 1953	Management and censorship of the media; oversight over global expansion of the Chinese media
Propaganda	**Cai Mingzhao**	Deputy Head, Party Central Committee Propaganda Department; Head, Party Central Committee External Propaganda Office; Director, State Council Information Office	Full Member of Party Central Committee	June 1955	Communist Party messaging for audiences outside China, including "guidance and coordination" of Chinese media reporting aimed at foreign audiences
Security	**Meng Jianzhu**	Party Secretary, Party Central Commission of Politics and Law	Member, Party Politburo; Full Member of Party Central Committee	July 1947	Security organs and the judiciary, including oversight over the Ministry of State Security, which is responsible for internal and external intelligence gathering and counter-intelligence
Security	**Guo Shengkun**	State Councilor; Deputy Party Secretary of Party Central Commission of Politics and Law; Minister and Party Secretary of Ministry of Public Security; Commissioner General of Police	Full Member of Party Central Committee; Member of State Council Party Committee	October 1954	Public security, including the police
Security	**Geng Huichang**	Minister of State Security	Full Member of Party Central Committee	November 1951	Internal and external intelligence gathering and counter-intelligence

Area of Responsibility	Name	Foreign Affairs-Related Position(s)	(Other) Communist Party Titles	Birthdate	Portfolio
Commerce	**Gao Hucheng**	Minister and Party Secretary, Ministry of Commerce	Full Member of Party Central Committee	August 1951	Domestic and foreign trade, inward and outward foreign investment, foreign aid
Taiwan Affairs	**Zhang Zhijun**	Director, Party Central Committee Taiwan Work Office; Minister, State Council Taiwan Affairs Office	Full Member of Party Central Committee	February 1953	Taiwan affairs, including interactions with other countries related to Taiwan
Hong Kong and Macao Affairs	**Wang Guangya**	Director, State Council Hong Kong and Macao Affairs Office	Full Member of Party Central Committee	March 1950	Policy related to the Chinese Special Administrative Regions of Hong Kong and Macao, including interactions with other countries related to Hong Kong and Macao
Overseas Chinese Affairs	**Qiu Yuanping**	Director and Party Secretary, Overseas Chinese Affairs Office of the State Council; Standing Committee Member, Chinese People's Political Consultative Conference National Committee		November 1953	Policies related to ethnic Chinese with foreign nationalities
National People's Congress (NPC)	**Fu Ying**	Chair, National People's Congress Foreign Affairs Committee; Member, NPC Standing Committee		January 1953	Advising on legislation related to foreign affairs and defense; international parliamentary exchanges.

Source: Xinhua News Agency biographies and ministry and office websites.

Leading Officials of the Ministry of Foreign Affairs

As **Table 2** shows, the Foreign Minister is one of many senior foreign policy players in China. He is outranked by the State Councilor for foreign affairs and frequently outmaneuvered by more powerful bureaucracies, such as those of the military and the security apparatus. Within the Foreign Ministry, the minister effectively shares power with the Executive Vice Minister, who holds the protocol rank of a full minister, and who heads the ministry's Communist Party Committee. The Executive Vice Minister is an alternate member of the Party Central Committee, while the minister is a full member.

Table 3. The Leadership of the Ministry of Foreign Affairs (as of 11/2013)

Listed in descending protocol rank order

Name	Foreign Affairs-Related Position	(Other) Communist Party Titles	Birthdate	Significant Previous Positions	Portfolio
Wang Yi	Minister of Foreign Affairs	Full Member of Party Central Committee; Presumed Deputy Party Secretary of Foreign Ministry Party Committee	October 1953	Director, Taiwan Work Office of the Party Central Committee and Minister, Taiwan Affairs Office of the State Council (2008-2013); Ambassador to Japan (2004-2007); Vice Minister of Foreign Affairs (2007-2008 and 2001-2004)	Leadership of the Ministry of Foreign Affairs
Zhang Yesui	Executive Vice Minister of Foreign Affairs	Alternate Member of Party Central Committee; Party Secretary of Foreign Ministry Party Committee	October 1953	Ambassador to the United States (2009-2012); Permanent Representative to the United Nations (2008-2009); Vice Minister of Foreign Affairs (2003-2008)	Party affairs and executive work of the ministry; Hong Kong, Macao and Taiwan-related foreign affairs
Song Tao	Vice Minister of Foreign Affairs	Unknown	April 1955	Ambassador to the Philippines (2007-2008); Director General, Department of Chinese Diplomatic Missions Abroad (2004-2007); Ambassador to Guyana (2002-2004)	Europe; retired ministry personnel; administration, finance, and Communist Party affairs for the ministry and diplomatic missions abroad

Name	Foreign Affairs-Related Position	(Other) Communist Party Titles	Birthdate	Significant Previous Positions	Portfolio
Li Baodong	Vice Minister of Foreign Affairs	Unknown	April 1955	Permanent Representative to the United Nations (2009-2013); Permanent Representative to the U.N. Office at Geneva and other international organizations in Switzerland (2006-2009); Ambassador to Zambia (2005-2006)	International organizations and conferences, international economic affairs, and arms control
Zhai Jun	Vice Minister of Foreign Affairs	Unknown	December 1954	Director General, Department of West Asian and North African Affairs (2003-2006); Ambassador to Libya (1997-2000)	West Asia and North Africa, Africa; information (overseeing spokespersons' office and management of China-based foreign journalists)
Cheng Guoping	Vice Minister of Foreign Affairs	Unknown	May 1952	Ambassador to Kazakhstan (2008-2009); Director-General, Department of European and Central Asian Affairs (2006-2008)	Europe-Central Asia, external security affairs, and foreign affairs management
Xie Hangsheng	Member of the Ministry of Foreign Affairs Leadership Team	Party Secretary, Ministry Communist Party Disciplinary Inspection Commission branch	January 1955	Ambassador to Denmark (2005-2011); Ambassador to Bulgaria (2002-2005)	Consular affairs; discipline inspection and supervision of ministry personnel
Liu Zhenmin	Vice Minister of Foreign Affairs	Unknown	August 1955	Permanent Representative to the U.N. Office at Geneva and other international organizations in Switzerland (2011-2013); Deputy Permanent Representative to the United Nations (2006-2009); Director General, Department of Treaty and Law (2003-2006)	Asia, treaties and laws, boundaries and oceanic affairs

Name	Foreign Affairs-Related Position	(Other) Communist Party Titles	Birthdate	Significant Previous Positions	Portfolio
Zhang Kunsheng	Assistant Minister of Foreign Affairs	Unknown	August 1958	Director-General, Ministry Protocol Department (2007-2011)	Latin America and the Caribbean, protocol, and translation and interpretation
Zhang Ming	Assistant Minister of Foreign Affairs	Unknown	June 1957	Director General, Ministry General Office (2010-2011); Director General, Department of African Affairs (2009-2010); Ambassador to Kenya and Permanent Representative to the U.N. Environment Program and UN-Habitat (2006-2009)	Ministry general office, personnel, and archives
Zheng Zeguang	Assistant Minister of Foreign Affairs	Member of Ministry Communist Party Committee	October 1963	Vice Mayor of Nanjing (2010-2013); Director General, Department of North American and Oceanian Affairs (2008-2010)	Policy planning, and North America and Oceania

Source: Website of Ministry of Foreign Affairs of the People's Republic of China, http://www.fmprc.gov.cn/mfa_chn/wjb_602314/zygy_602330/; database of Communist Party Congresses on the Communist Party of China's web portal, http://cpc.people.com.cn/GB/64162/64168/351850/index.html.

Notes: The Foreign Ministry does not publicly disclose the full membership of its Communist Party Committee. Zheng Zeguang is the only top Foreign Ministry official whose public biography discloses membership of the Ministry Party Committee. Confirmation of Zhang Yesui's position as Party Secretary of the Foreign Ministry Party Committee is contained in State Council of the PRC, *State Council General Office Notice Regarding the Establishment of a Leading Small Group for the First National Geographic Census* (in Chinese), June 13, 2013, http://www.gov.cn/zwgk/2013-06/13/content_2425368.htm.

Author Contact Information

Susan V. Lawrence
Specialist in Asian Affairs
slawrence@crs.loc.gov, 7-2577

Acknowledgments

The author is grateful to CRS Graphics Specialist Jamie Hutchinson for creating the graphics in this report and to CRS User Support Specialist Claudia Guidi and CRS Editor Shelley Harlan for their assistance with the report's formatting.

www.ingramcontent.com/pod-product-compliance
Lightning Source LLC
Chambersburg PA
CBHW080750290526
45790CB00008B/3397